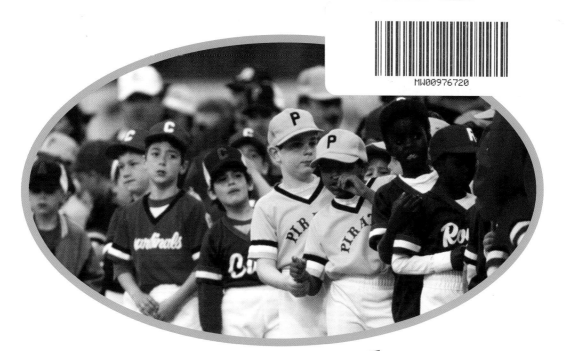

Baseball Math

BY ERIN SULLIVAN

Table of Contents

How Do You Get Ready for a Baseball Game?

There are millions of baseball fans all over the world. Lots of these fans are kids. They love going to **Major League** games, trading baseball cards, and reading about their favorite players. Many boys and girls also play on **Little League** teams.

Most Little League ▶ teams play about fifteen games per season.

You need at least 9 players to make a baseball team. But most Little League teams have between 12 and 15 players. Imagine that there are 3 Little League teams in your town. If you put 10 kids on each team, how many kids in all will be playing baseball?

10 + 10 + 10 = _____ players

If you put 12 players on each team, how many kids in all will be playing baseball?

12 + 12 + 12 = _____ players

Little League baseball is a lot like Major League baseball. In both leagues, there are nine different positions on the field, including a pitcher and a catcher. Batters in both leagues try to get on base so they can score runs for their team.

There are also differences between the leagues. One difference is in the distance between the bases. In Little League, the bases are 60 feet apart.

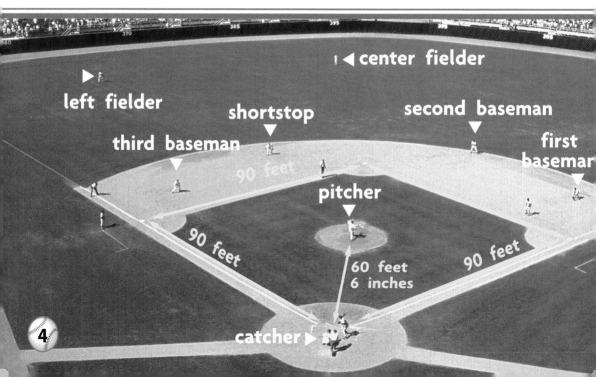

center fielder

left fielder

shortstop

second baseman

third baseman

first baseman

90 feet

pitcher

90 feet

60 feet 6 inches

90 feet

catcher

In the Major League, the bases are 90 feet apart. If a Major Leaguer hits a home run, this number sentence shows how many feet he runs:

90 + 90 + 90 + 90 = 360 feet.

What does the number sentence look like when a Little Leaguer hits a home run? What is the difference between how far a Major League player runs and how far a Little League player runs?

right fielder

The infield is known as the diamond because of its diamond shape. First, second, and third bases are white bags that are fifteen inches wide.

Little League players and Major League players practice a lot for their games. Major League players go through spring training. Little League players usually have practices a few times each week.

Below is the practice schedule for a Little League team named the Mustangs. The chart shows when each practice starts and how long it lasts. Can you figure out what time each practice will end?

MUSTANGS

Team Practice Schedule

	Start Time	Practice Length	End Time
Monday	4:30 p.m.	1 hour	
Wednesday	3:00 p.m.	2 hours	
Friday	5:15 p.m.	1 ½ hours	

At baseball practices, players do exercises such as sit-ups and push-ups to develop their muscles. They practice sprinting and running to improve their speed. They also practice baseball skills such as throwing, catching, and fielding a ball.

Fast Pitch
One of the greatest pitchers of all time is Nolan Ryan. In 1974, one of his pitches was clocked at 100.9 miles per hour!

Nolan Ryan

One special tool that many players use to practice their batting is a pitching machine. The machine pitches a number of balls in a row so that the batter can practice without a real pitcher. Imagine that you use a pitching machine and hit 3 balls every minute. If you hit for 5 minutes, the number sentence would look like this:

3 + 3 + 3 + 3 + 3 = 15 balls.

How many balls would you hit in 10 minutes? What would your number sentence look like?

What Happens at a Baseball Game?

It is exciting to play in a Little League game. But it is also exciting to watch one. Moms and dads, brothers and sisters, grandparents, and friends will often show up to sit in the **bleachers**, or benches, and cheer on the players.

One way to find out how many fans there are at a game is to count each person. Another way is to count up the number of people on each bleacher and then skip count by the number of bleachers. How many fans are at this Mustangs game?

Another great part of going to a Little League game is getting snacks. You can find a snack cart at every Mustangs game. It sells treats such as hot dogs, potato chips, ice cream, and soda pop.

How much money would it cost if you bought a hot dog, a pretzel, and a bottle of water?

$_____ for a hot dog + $_____ for a pretzel + $_____ for a bottle of water = $_____

HOT DOG $1.50 + PRETZEL $1.25 + WATER $1.00 = ?

If you had $5.00 to spend, how much change would you get? Would you have enough money to buy an ice pop?

Sam's Snack Cart Menu

	Hot Dog	$1.50
	Chili Dog	$2.00
	Potato Chips	$.75
	Pretzel	$1.25
	Cookie	$.50
	Popsicle	$1.00
	Water	$1.00
	Juice	$1.25
	Soda Pop	$1.25

Hot Dogs
Soda

$5 $5
$5
$5 $5

13

Once the game begins, all eyes are on the field. A batter steps up to home plate. The pitcher throws the ball. Maybe the batter will get a single and run to first base. Maybe she will hit a home run and go around all the bases!

But if the pitch is good and the batter swings and misses, it is a strike. If the pitch is not good and the batter doesn't swing at it, then it's a ball.

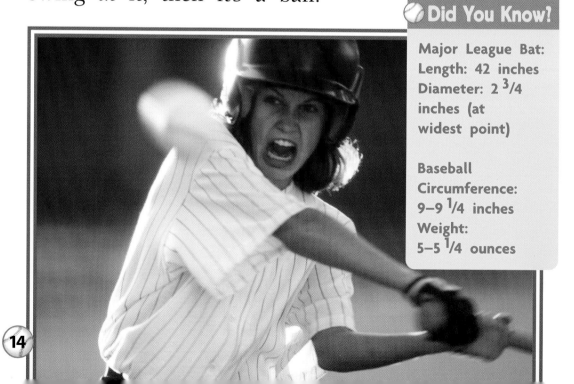

Did You Know?

Major League Bat:
Length: 42 inches
Diameter: $2\frac{3}{4}$ inches (at widest point)

Baseball Circumference: $9-9\frac{1}{4}$ inches
Weight: $5-5\frac{1}{4}$ ounces

Players keep track of how often they get a hit when they are at bat. This number is called a **batting average.**

A player's batting average is found by dividing the number of times the player gets a hit by the number of times the player is at bat. Look at these players' batting averages. Who is hitting the best this season? The worst?

MUSTANGS

⭐ Player Batting Averages ⭐			
Player	Hits	At-Bats	Batting Average
Jed	13	65	.200
Wendy	16	64	.250
Olivia	17	51	.333

Great Hitters
Baseball great Ted Williams once said that the best players hit the ball only 3 out of every 10 times at bat! One of the greatest hitters of all time was Babe Ruth. His batting average was .342.

Major League baseball games have nine **innings**. Most Little League games last six innings. During each inning, both teams get a chance to bat. If the score is tied at the end of six innings, the game usually goes into extra innings.

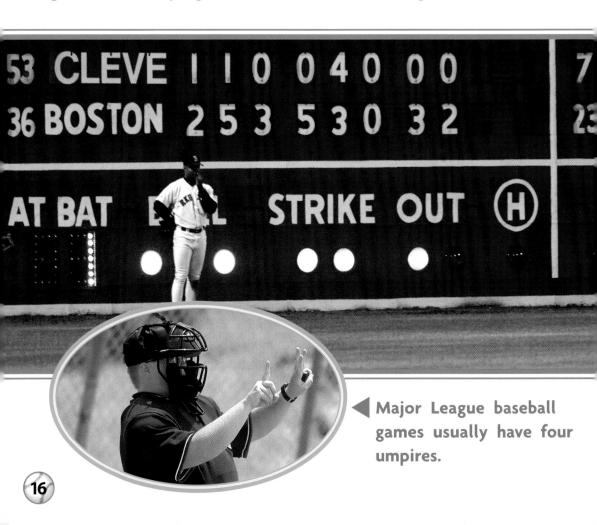

| 53 CLEVE | I | I | 0 | 0 | 4 | 0 | 0 | 0 | 7 |
| 36 BOSTON | 2 | 5 | 3 | 5 | 3 | 0 | 3 | 2 | 23 |

AT BAT ___ STRIKE OUT (H)

◄ Major League baseball games usually have four umpires.

The scoreboard below shows the results of a game between the Mustangs and the Blue Sox. To find the final score, add up the runs that each team scored in each inning. Who was winning after the third inning? What was the score then? Who won the game? What was the final score?

Inning	1	2	3	4	5	6
Mustangs	0	1	2	3	2	2
Blue Sox	0	0	4	3	1	1

The Longest Game

The longest Major League game on record was between the Chicago White Sox and the Milwaukee Brewers in 1984. The game had twenty-five innings and lasted eight hours and six minutes!

▲ Since 1959, the Little League World Series has been played in Williamsport, Pennsylvania.

After the regular Little League season is over, the best teams go on to compete in the Little League **World Series**.

The chart below shows the Little League teams with the most World Series wins. Can you turn this information into a bar graph?

Winner	Number of Wins
Taiwan	16
California	5
New Jersey, Pennsylvania	4
Japan, Mexico	3
New York, South Korea, Texas	2

Baseball Math Answers

Page 3

With 10 players on a team, 30 kids; with 12 players on a team, 36 kids

Page 5

60 + 60 + 60 + 60 = 240 feet; 120 feet

Page 7

Monday at 5:30 p.m.; Wednesday at 5:00 p.m.; Friday at 6:45 p.m.

Page 9

30 balls in 10 minutes;
3 + 3 + 3 + 3 + 3 + 3 + 3 + 3 + 3 + 3 = 30 balls

Page 11

8 x 10 = 80 fans

Page 12

$1.50 + $1.25 + $1.00 = $3.75; change from $5.00 would be $1.25; yes Popsicles cost $1.00.

Page 15

Olivia at .333; Jed at .200

Page 17

Blue Sox; 4 to 3; Mustangs; 10 to 9

Page 18

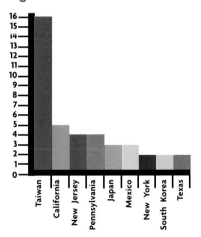

Glossary

batting average (BAT-tihng AV-uh-rihj): a number that shows how often a batter gets a hit when he or she is at bat

bleachers (BLEE-cherz): benches where fans sit during a baseball game

innings (IH-ningz): rounds in a baseball game, during which both teams get to bat

Little League (LIH-tuhl LEEG): a group of baseball teams for players age 5 to 18

Major League (MAY-johr LEEG): a group of professional baseball teams

World Series (WERLD SEER-eez): a final tournament for baseball teams with the best season records

Index